THEN & NOW

VANDERGRIFT

D1717146

Opposite: Here is a historic image of Vandergrift as viewed from across the Kiskiminetas River. Rolling hills can be seen in the distance. Where the Townsend farm used to lie, the winding streets of newly established Vandergrift slope down toward the river. To the far left is Hamilton Avenue, and to its right are Jefferson, Columbia, and Farragut Avenues, respectively. Just beyond the town is an open area with a grove of trees and the settlement of Vandergrift Heights.

VANDERGRIFT

Sara McGuire

*This book is dedicated to all those who made Vandergrift
what it was in its heyday and to those who are working
to restore the town today.*

Library of Congress Control Number: 2008941206

Published by Arcadia Publishing
Charleston SC, Chicago IL, Portsmouth NH, San Francisco CA

Printed in the United States of America

For all general information contact Arcadia Publishing at:
Telephone 843-853-2070
Fax 843-853-0044
E-mail sales@arcadiapublishing.com
For customer service and orders:
Toll-Free 1-888-313-2665

Visit us on the Internet at www.arcadiapublishing.com

On the front cover: These festively decorated houses at the corner of Hancock and Adams Avenues create a sense of Vandergrift's small-town atmosphere. Like most rural communities, it has been built up through the hard work of its citizens and includes quiet tree-lined streets, parks, baseball fields, and family owned businesses. However, beneath its small-town exterior, Vandergrift is innovative and distinct, as anyone who takes the time to learn more about the town will realize. (Historic image courtesy of Victorian Vandergrift Museum and Historical Society; contemporary image, author's collection.)

On the back cover: Sherman Avenue is an example of Vandergrift's originality. Trees line the street in this historic image, showing the rounded avenues and greenery that Frederick Law Olmsted's firm intended for the town. To the left, the Sherman Inn can be seen. To the right, although not visible in this image, the Vandergrift Block building begins at the corner of Sherman Avenue and stretches up Washington Avenue. The Sherman Inn was meant for Vandergrift's early visitors, and the Vandergrift Block building included business and living space. (Courtesy of Victorian Vandergrift Museum and Historical Society.)

CONTENTS

ACKNOWLEDGMENTS

When asked to do this project, I was excited and apprehensive about completing it. Having always lived in Vandergrift, I thought that I knew the town and more popular bits of its history fairly well. However, researching and collecting images for this book has taught me much more about Vandergrift's past and its significance. I would like to thank everyone who has helped me with this project so that I could learn these lessons, and I hope that I successfully pass them on to those who read Then & Now: *Vandergrift*. Hopefully, I have not left anyone out, but if I have, accept my apologies and know that, even if not mentioned, your help was still appreciated.

All of the older images were provided by the Victorian Vandergrift Museum and Historical Society (VVMHS) and the Vandergrift Improvement Program (VIP) unless otherwise noted. All of the images showing the town in its present state were taken by me, the author. I want to thank Beth Caporali, Bill Hesketh, Mary Jane Slicker, and others at the VVMHS for allowing me to look through its collection of images. I also want to thank Sherry Jenks for her proofreading efforts and Shaun Yurcaba, the main street coordinator with Pittsburgh History and Landmarks Foundation for the VIP, for guiding me during this process.

Many others have offered their help. Without them, this book would have been missing some of its more unique images and information. Charlene Hoffer of the Vandergrift Public Library, Norman Myers of Myers Print Shop, and Gabe Cole of Buttermilk Falls Printing Company became other sources of historic photographs. Poppy Basile of Sweetlane Chocolate Shop took the time to sit with me one afternoon, and I truly enjoyed hearing the stories she shared as well as seeing her photographs of the shop. Jim Cibik, Kurt Dunmire, and Rosemary Ferrante provided me with more photographs and information about Vandergrift's businesses. I thank them for the time that they gave to me, as well as Kenneth Blose for being a source of information. I also thank Rev. F. Neal Galley, Pastor Karen Lovelace, Anthony Nicholas, and Rev. Kathleen Taylor for being so welcoming and allowing me to interview them about their churches. Mostly I thank my family for their support throughout this project. This has been a wonderful opportunity for me to become reacquainted with my hometown and develop new acquaintances with those who have helped me to complete this book.

INTRODUCTION

A pamphlet printed for the Vandergrift Chamber of Commerce in the 1930s states, "Vandergrift is the culmination of a dream." The town was founded in 1895, but the dream that led to this point had its beginnings in a much earlier time. The individual responsible for this dream entered onto the scene in 1886. At that time, George Gibson McMurtry became the manager of the Apollo Iron and Steel Company located in Apollo, a town southeast of Vandergrift. The plant thrived as a manufacturer of galvanized iron with McMurtry as its director, and he was soon looking for a site for the establishment of another plant. The site he considered was a beautiful piece of farmland down the Kiskiminetas River from Apollo. He bought the 640-acre Townsend farm as well as the Hugh Jones, Laufer, and Varner farms in 1892. The next year, workers at the Apollo Iron and Steel Company went on strike. They felt they deserved higher pay than what had been agreed upon in a national union contract. In the meantime, land near the Apollo mill was purchased by two individuals planning on reselling it to the mill at a much higher price. In 1894, McMurtry's desire for expansion, the strike, and a higher buying price for nearby land led him to finally begin to move forward with plans for the farmland he had purchased.

One can only imagine what the land where Vandergrift now rests looked like in the past. In the 17th and 18th centuries, it was home to Delaware Indian settlements and then cleared for farming. It was in this state that McMurtry first viewed the site. This parcel of land juts into the path of the Kiskiminetas River, which wraps itself around the seeming peninsula of hilly earth. What McMurtry meant for this land was not just a plant and accompanying grimy industrial town with rows of generic houses following a grid plan that was the common atmosphere of mill towns of his time. In a letter addressed to landscape designer Frederick Law Olmsted in 1895 requesting his services in designing McMurtry's dream town, Apollo Iron and Steel Company treasurer Wallace Bache made it clear that the town was to break free of the trends of the day. He writes, "We desire to have a town that in many features will be unique, and in all respects more attractive than the average manufacturing town of the present day. In fact, we want something better than the best." Like other industrialists, McMurtry wanted to make a profit, but he knew the key to the success of his business would be healthy and contented workers. Therefore, the town he was setting out to create was to have all the comforts his employees could need.

In developing his plans, McMurtry traveled to industrial settlements throughout the United States as well as towns in Belgium, England, France, Germany, and Russia. After doing this research, he decided to call upon Olmsted, Olmsted and Eliot, the design firm of Frederick Law Olmsted. Olmsted had famously designed New York City's Central Park, incorporating his ideal of creating green space in urban areas, a conception fitting only too perfectly with what McMurtry wanted for his town. Olmsted, Olmsted and Eliot agreed to work with McMurtry, and the dream began to take shape. The town was named Vandergrift after Capt. Jacob J. Vandergrift, a personal friend of McMurtry's and the main stockholder for the Apollo Iron and Steel Company. It was also called a "workingman's paradise" in 1901 by *Iron Age Magazine* because of the setting and standard of living it offered the mill workers.

From these beginnings, Vandergrift has gone through a series of changes. Horse-drawn wagons no longer rumble down yellow brick streets, passenger trains no longer bring visitors to the Sherman Inn, and shops have changed hands as well as appearance. One innovation that has significantly changed Vandergrift is the automobile. With the development of cars, people found that they could travel farther outside of town to get what they needed, and as a result, Vandergrift's businesses have suffered. In this, Vandergrift is like many of America's small towns. Although some have left, many have stayed, aware that there is still something special about this place. Today people rush forward into the ever-faster pace of the future all the while wishing for the slow-paced life of the past, a time when friends and family visited one another on Sundays and grocery shopping meant entering into aroma-filled shops where the goods were always fresh. Elements of this past lifestyle can still be found in small-town America. In his desire to make Vandergrift a green community while still wanting the town to have all of the technological innovations of the day, McMurtry's vision reflects present concerns. Thus, Vandergrift was ahead of its time and continues to look to the future while attempting to restore the past.

ROLLING HILLS TO WINDING STREETS

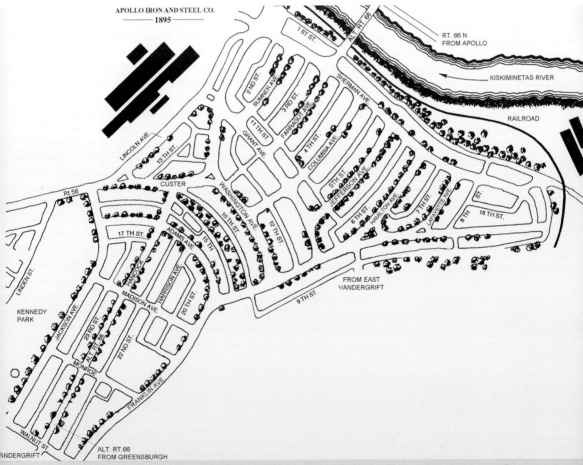

The design firm of Olmsted, Olmsted and Eliot was called upon by George Gibson McMurtry to create a layout following the contours of the land. Anyone who walks down Vandergrift's streets or looks at the town from across the Kiskiminetas River will clearly see that the streets flow into one another rather than forming sharp corners. This makes walking or driving through the town and views of Vandergrift's architecture even more pleasing. (Courtesy of Cliff McGuire.)

This historic photograph was taken in 1895. It depicts a site known as Rabbit Hill on the Riggle farm. The man standing along the fence has stopped his wagon just beyond the tree to the right as if he could not help looking out on the field with its haystacks. The road was supposedly a rocky one. It led to a small cemetery with only about eight graves. (Historic image courtesy of the Vandergrift Public Library.)

The photographer for this image was standing just to the right of where the Vandergrift mill was built and where Sherman Avenue still curves into Lincoln Avenue. Construction for the mill began early in Vandergrift's history, so one can easily imagine that the men and horse-drawn wagons were coming from the construction site that was to the left. Looking on the present scene, the train and freight stations are visible. (Historic image courtesy of Norman Myers.)

Taken on July 4, 1896, probably from the base of what is now Howell Street, this image gives a view over an area of town that came to be known as the Park Plan in 1907. The new mill can be seen in the distance. The area of the Park Plan is situated just to the west of what was a grove of trees and what is now Kennedy Park and Davis Field. It was named because of a baseball park located there and provided more housing lots for Vandergrift's quickly growing population. Linden Street, still paved with red bricks, became the main business district for Park Plan residents. (Historic image courtesy of the Vandergrift Public Library.)

Another image from July 4, 1896, this photograph shows people on their way down to or away from the Grove at the right. The Grove was a popular spot, especially on occasions such as the Fourth of July. It must have been raining that day because many of the women appear with umbrellas, although it is equally possible that they are trying to protect themselves from the sun. Rain or shine, everyone seems to have enjoyed an opportunity to visit the Grove. (Historic image courtesy of the Vandergrift Public Library.)

The Grove was a tree-lined valley, stretching from the Vandergrift Heights to Custer Avenue. A spring ran through the valley's center, and paths were forged along the sloping sides. There were picnic tables, a pavilion for band concerts, and rope swings. In 1919, the mill, having ownership of the Grove, proposed filling the valley with its excess ash and then creating a level park area for Vandergrift's residents. The proposal was agreed to, and the Grove was filled and leveled, becoming Kennedy Park and Davis Field.

Within Olmsted, Olmsted and Eliot's plan for Vandergrift was an attempt to maintain some of the greenery that the town was replacing. This was to be done through the incorporation of small parks into the town's layout. These were located throughout the town, and many remain today. Here is a view of the main park area, stretching up from the train station to the pedimented Casino Theatre building at the top. This space now provides an area for extra parking when the town is especially busy or when there is a show at the Casino Theatre.

This is another small park that still adorns the town. Franklin Avenue comes down on the right, and Hamilton Avenue branches off to the left. The triangular piece of land that the meeting of these two streets creates is not well suited for a building of any sort. Frederick Law Olmsted's firm made use of it by turning it into a green space. George Gibson McMurtry made Count Van Aubery, an arboriculturist from Germany, responsible for Vandergrift's planting beds and the trees lining the streets. Today the Vandergrift Garden Club maintains these park areas. (Historic image courtesy of Norman Myers.)

Looking up Grant Avenue, downtown Vandergrift appears to have been a very busy place at the dawn of the 20th century. Grant Avenue, like all of the avenues in Vandergrift proper, was paved with yellow brick and lined with cut stone curbs. These curbs remain throughout the town. McMurtry had intended Washington Avenue to be the main street in the business district, but the size of the lots made them more expensive. As a result, men with higher-paying jobs at the mill bought the larger properties on Washington Avenue and built beautiful homes for themselves and their families.

Many businesses decided to buy land on Grant and Columbia Avenues instead of purchasing the large, high-cost lots of Washington Avenue. The upper, residential part of Grant Avenue retains its original narrow width. The lower portion (shown here) had broad sidewalks, which were narrowed in the late 1920s, making Grant Avenue much wider than it was originally to allow for automobile traffic.

At one time, both sides of Columbia Avenue were lined with businesses, but it too had to be altered to accommodate for automobile traffic downtown. A number of stores along one side of the street were torn down and replaced by a parking lot in the 1960s. The intersection of Columbia and Grant Avenues, the site from which these images were taken, originally was the only point in Vandergrift proper where two streets met at a right angle.

Vandergrift boasts being one of the first worker-owned industrial communities in the United States. In June 1896, McMurtry announced the sale of lots. He waited until the town was completely laid out, sewage pipes installed, and utilities ready to be tapped into before making this announcement. Here the construction of Shingle Row on Sherman Avenue can be seen in 1897. Although these houses were built based on the same plan, many more residents built their homes to their own unique tastes and desires.

The George Gibson McMurtry Fire Hall, or No. 1 Fire Hall, located on Franklin Avenue, erected this arch across Lincoln Avenue for a parade around 1900. The firemen, identified by the "G.G.M.M.1" on their uniforms, have just come through the archway and are flanked on either side by carts with fire hoses. This firehouse was established in the fall of 1897. (Historic image courtesy of Norman Myers.)

At one time, Lincoln Avenue stretched outside of Vandergrift in the form of a narrow dirt road lined with houses. Later, this extension was widened, creating the need to demolish some of the houses. The roadway was renamed State Route 56. It leads out of Vandergrift and at one time was to become a more direct route to Pittsburgh. Its purpose was to provide such access to other towns and cities, but it contributes to the diversion of traffic from Vandergrift's downtown businesses.

This is a photograph of Hancock Avenue
in 1938. There are not many Vandergrift
residents who relish the fairly steep
climb of this street after a snowstorm. To
this day, Hancock maintains its position
as the major avenue joining Vandergrift
Heights with Vandergrift proper.
Vandergrift Heights, situated on the
hillside above Vandergrift, was a town
apart, begun at about the same time
as George Gibson McMurtry's dream
town. Vandergrift Heights, however,
did not have the design aesthetics and
commodities that Vandergrift proper
had. The two remained separate towns
until 1915.

Vandergrift Heights was mainly settled by Italian immigrants. Unlike Vandergrift proper, the streets in the heights were not curved, paved with yellow brick, or lined with cut stone sidewalks. Rather, there were dirt streets and boardwalks. Emerson Street, shown here around 1909, was one such roadway. While the avenues in Vandergrift proper were named for famous American presidents or generals and those in the Park Plan were named for trees, the streets in Vandergrift Heights were named for poets and authors. (Historic image courtesy of Bonnie McGuire.)

ROLLING HILLS TO WINDING STREETS

Before and after Vandergrift Heights became a part of Vandergrift proper in 1915, many heights residents established businesses on Longfellow Street. This meant that people of the heights could benefit from an array of shops closer to home than those on Grant Avenue. Someone walking along Longfellow Street in the 1920s would have passed by Ramer's Department Store, Arcadia Theater, Manganello's Fruit Market, Milie Brothers' Real Estate and Insurance, the Great Atlantic and Pacific Tea Company, as well as the Wilson and Longfellow Elementary Schools.

John Montgomery bought the land that eventually became East Vandergrift from William Penn's sons in 1773. It came to be governed by nearby Allegheny Township and was called Morning Sun. In the last decade of the 19th century, the land was purchased by W. S. Beamer, who divided it to resell as lots to mill workers. On December 18, 1901, Morning Sun became East Vandergrift Borough and still remains a separate town. The historic image shows it as it appeared on March 18, 1936, after the great St. Patrick's Day flood. (Historic image courtesy of VVMHS, photograph by F. Lloyd Earhart.)

The Vandergrift Bridge crosses the Kiskiminetas River and leads traffic to and from Vandergrift proper and North Vandergrift. Before a bridge was built here, people regularly traveled back and forth by boat. In 1900, the first bridge was built and is shown here in this historic image. A second bridge was built in 1932, and the third and final bridge appears in the modern photograph.

Levi Stitt was the initial occupant of land just to the northeast of Vandergrift on the other side of the Kiskiminetas River. He and his brother John Franz Stitt managed a flour mill located on Stitt's Run Road. Beginning in 1898, Levi Stitt laid out his land for the settlement of mill workers. This settlement became North Vandergrift. The photograph of flood wreckage shown at the intersection of North Vandergrift's First and Lincoln Avenues was taken on March 18, 1936. (Historic image courtesy of VVMHS, photograph by F. Lloyd Earhart.)

CHAPTER 2

VANDERGRIFT'S OTHER VISIONARIES

The workers of the number five mill sat for this photograph on August 18, 1913. Pictured from left to right are (first row) unidentified, J. Welsh, James Sutherland, J. Newhouse, W. Rakustraw, and ? Davis; (second row) four unidentified, ? Stanley, unidentified, unidentified, S. Kunkle, and H. McCollough. George Gibson McMurtry and Olmsted, Olmsted and Eliot may have planned Vandergrift, but it was these men and their families who made the town a reality and gave it character. After their intense work shifts at the mill, they went to the mill's greenhouse and selected something to plant while walking home.

Vandergrift's train station, pictured here in 1910, saw the arrival of many of the town's visionary citizens. The settlers of Vandergrift proper were mostly English, German, Scottish, Irish, and Greek. The immigrants who settled in the Park Plan and Vandergrift Heights were mainly Italian, and those who moved into North Vandergrift were mostly of Polish, Lithuanian, Slovak, and African American descent. The station now functions as the law offices of Caroselli, Spagnolli, and Beachler.

VANDERGRIFT'S OTHER VISIONARIES

The 1920s photograph shows Leonard G. Elswick's American Railway Express truck loaded down with supplies from the freight station (right). Elswick can be seen standing in the second row, sixth from the left. He was a caterer as well as working at the American Railway Express and Vandergrift Airport. He was also owner of the Kiski Theater on Grant Avenue for a time. Just as the train station no longer receives passengers, the freight station no longer operates according to its original purpose. It is now the site of Spaniel's Beer Distributor.

On October 29, 1895, Apollo Iron and Steel Company's Vandergrift plant rolled its first iron, and on January 11, 1897, it made its first steel. From these firsts, the plant went on to produce steel for the Gateway Arch in St. Louis and finish and polish steel for the Unisphere in New York City. On January 1, 1951, when bought by U.S. Steel Company, the plant began specializing in electrical sheets. The mill was forced to close in 1988 but shortly reopened under Allegheny Ludlum Steel.

VANDERGRIFT'S OTHER VISIONARIES

Vandergrift's foundry was begun at the same time as the mill. It produced the necessary steel, iron, and brass parts for the rolling of sheets at the plant. In 1901, the foundry was purchased by the United Engineer and Foundry Company. While the plant was responsible for the casting of the gate hinges of the Panama Canal, Vandergrift's foundry was the creator of the cylinders attached to chains in the canal to impede ships from coming too close to the gates. The foundry is now operated by Metal Service Company Incorporated.

The George McMurtry Fire Hall was named for McMurtry after he donated land and the first equipment to the department. It included the office for Dr. Joseph O'Brien's Rainbow Control Service, an emergency system he developed that included Vandergrift and surrounding towns. Each fire company chose a different color for its equipment, and the office in this fire hall controlled 17 fire departments, 14 police departments, 5 ambulance services, and 3 search-and-rescue units. O'Brien traveled the United States explaining how the Rainbow Control Service worked and in this way developed a prototype for 911. (Historic image courtesy of Norman Myers.)

CHAPTER 3

SERVICES FOR EVERY NEED

A band stands in front of the Vandergrift Savings and Trust Company within the first two decades of the 1900s. It was here that Vandergrift's residents placed the money they worked so hard to earn. In 1916, this amounted to over $1 million, according to Ida Tarbell, a journalist of business practices and the early history of George Gibson McMurtry and Vandergrift.

This is a slightly later historic image of the Vandergrift Savings and Trust Company. In June 1897, McMurtry began the First National Bank of Vandergrift in the Vandergrift Block building along Washington Avenue. However, it could not satisfy the needs for loans in a growing town. As a result, in 1902, the Vandergrift Savings and Trust Company took its place. In 1905, the company moved to this building, designed by architect James E. Allison, at the corner of Grant and Washington Avenues.

The Anchor Building is curved to follow the path of Washington Avenue as it moves into Columbia Avenue. It was named for the anchor symbol carved at its top as well as for its purpose. It was supposed to anchor the business district originally planned for Washington Avenue, which developed on Grant Avenue instead. The Anchor Building has been the home of many businesses, including a clothing store, grocery, and, more recently, an insurance group.

The Vandergrift Land and Improvement Company announced the sale of lots on June 8, 1896. It offered prospective residents a choice of 814 different plots of land, 200 being reserved for business use. The Vandergrift Laundry Company took up a site that is now the parking lot above Occasions or Buttermilk Falls Printing Company. Although no clearer identification remains, it is known that the names of the figures at left are Thurman Jackson, Paul Means, and E. J. Walcott, who was the laundry's manager. The last girl standing on the right is Anna Kepple White.

SERVICES FOR EVERY NEED

Moore Photography Studio came to occupy the lot at 134 Washington Avenue. A. W. Moore must have only recently finished the building's construction because a temporary fabric sign identifies him as the occupant. This studio is responsible for quite a few of the historic photographs that appear in this book, such as the view of Vandergrift on the title page, as well as the images of the foundry, Armstrong Furniture, and the Pennington and Son building. This building is now occupied by the Fireman's Club.

H. J. Kuhns' plumbing shop was located at 123 Washington Avenue. The building's facade has been greatly simplified and it is now the home of Hansen's Allstate Insurance Agency. The painted sign on the side of the original building read "H. J. Kuhns, Sanitary Plumbing, Gas Fitting, Hot Water and Steam Heating." Presently, the open lot above this business is occupied by Frank's Place, while the building below is now home to A. J.'s Restaurant and Lounge.

SERVICES FOR EVERY NEED

A primary example of a family owned business, Robert Armstrong built Armstrong Furniture on Washington Avenue in 1903. R. W. Dunmire worked in Armstrong's shop beginning in 1919 and then took over the furniture store in 1937. His son Jack Dunmire worked in the store all of his life before passing it on to his son Kurt Dunmire, who continues to maintain the business. (Historic image courtesy of Kurt Dunmire.)

The Phillips Brothers Garage, shown here in 1905, was a service and repair station. In addition, it was an ambulance service. At a later date, this building became Brock's Motors, which sold Dodge and Plymouth automobiles but also made a profit out of offering tickets for Edwards Bus Line. Just below this building was the Vandergrift Block building, which was demolished in 1965. It was a structure that supported a number of the town's earliest necessary offices.

The building immediately
to the right of the Anchor
Building is shown in this
image from before 1905. At
the time that the photograph
was taken, it housed the
offices of a Dr. Schaull and
a Dr. McLaughlin. Patients
could visit their offices and
then, if necessary, walk
a couple of doors down
to the Vandergrift Drug
Company. While some of
the upper-story porches on
Vandergrift's downtown
buildings have been
removed, this one has been
expanded. (Historic image
courtesy of Norman Myers.)

This photograph from around 1900 shows three storefronts on Columbia Avenue. From left to right are a tailor, the Vandergrift Drug Company, and a store that sold tablewares and chandeliers. R. Norman Myers Jr. bought the corner store in 1930 and moved his printing business here from across the street. Norman Myers III bought the business from his father in 1975 and extended the shop in the 1980s into what was the drug company. Originally, there were apartments upstairs, but now this space serves as Myers Keeping Rooms Bed and Breakfast. (Historic image courtesy of Norman Myers.)

SERVICES FOR EVERY NEED

At one time, a portion of this building served as Sam Calderone's fruit market, and the other part was John Secreto's shoe repair shop. The historic image is from the 1960s before the building was torn down. The full parking spaces lining the street signal that there was a need for more parking areas. Once this building came down, the land that it occupied fulfilled that purpose by becoming a small parking lot. (Historic image courtesy of Norman Myers.)

The Diamond Store building appears here as it would have looked in the first few decades of the 20th century. It curves down from Columbia Avenue onto Grant Avenue, as it still does today. However, major differences have been made to this building's facade. Also, where it once provided room for numerous businesses, it now provides space for only one. Presently, it is occupied by First Commonwealth Bank.

SERVICES FOR EVERY NEED

This building lies at the intersection of Grant and Columbia Avenues. It is diagonal to the old Diamond Store building. When this photograph was taken in the early 1900s, the main floor was occupied by Phillips Brothers Jewelers and Opticians. Nicodemus Real Estate and Insurance was also located here. Today it houses the law offices of Uncapher, Uncapher, and Fox.

Directly behind the men and wagon is 146 Grant Avenue, a storefront that was owned by S. M. McGahey in 1905. It was added onto to create the present building at the same site, now occupied by Malcolm's Quality Clothes. Just above this, at 148 Grant Avenue, the historic image shows H. J. Gerner's ice cream, soda fountain, and bakery. To the right of McGahey's shop was Thomas W. Murphy's drugstore.

The building featured in this historic photograph shows H. G. Phillips's shop (left) and W. C. Tomlinson's shop (right). Phillips advertises watches, optical goods, repairing, jewelry, and diamonds, while Tomlinson promotes cigars, prescriptions, and stationery. The Vandergrift Improvement Program office is now located in Phillips's store, and Dave's Appliance is in Tomlinson's. The storefront to the far left was the location of a J. C. Penney store. This building is now being restored and rehabilitated by the Vandergrift Improvement Program.

Several feet of snow coated Vandergrift in this 1950 photograph. None of the shops that appear here along Grant Avenue remain today; instead, they have all been replaced with a new variety of businesses. There has always been an assortment of services. From 1919 to 1923, Vandergrift had 5 pharmacies, 21 stores with food products, 15 general stores, 9 shoe stores, 8 restaurants, and 8 ice cream or candy stores. (Historic image courtesy of Norman Myers.)

SERVICES FOR EVERY NEED

Vandergrift's first post office opened on August 20, 1896. The postmaster at the time was Henry Nichols. On February 1, 1897, it became a part of the Vandergrift Block building. Several years later, John Adams and George Hamilton became the town's first mail carriers, beginning their deliveries on September 1, 1902. This image shows the new post office on Farragut Avenue shortly after it was dedicated in 1936.

The 1950 snowfall makes an appearance again in this photograph of the G. C. Murphy 5 and 10¢ store. The building's creaking wooden floor and pressed metal ceiling still remain characteristic features today. An assortment of household items, stationary, candy, toys, clothing, and other general items were laid out on shelves and display tables for customers. Just inside the door was a large popcorn machine. The shop is again alive with variety, as it has recently reopened as Pampered Puppies, a pet store that also offers grooming services. (Historic image courtesy of Norman Myers.)

Taken on January 9, 1908, the Pennington and Son building is shown after a fire. The Vandergrift Commercial College had moved to the second story of this building only two years before. This college provided a number of business-related classes. In 1924, it offered a college preparatory course, as well as classes in electricity, mathematics, garage and automobile accounting, and mechanical drawing. Shortly after 1924, the college closed down. In spite of the burnt-out interior, the structure was rebuilt and is still located along Grant Avenue.

As can be seen in the pediment of the earlier photograph, this was the Independent Order of Odd Fellows (IOOF) building. The IOOF was just one of the many fraternal organizations that established itself in Vandergrift. These organizations included the George McMurtry Fire Hall, or No. 1 Fire Hall, and the No. 2 Fire Hall in Vandergrift Heights as well as veterans and civic groups. The building is now the home of Ross Pharmacy, the Good News Center, and an accountant's office.

Peter and Poppy Basile bought what became Sweetlane Chocolate Shop in 1952. It had been a restaurant and was richly decorated with mahogany wall paneling, booths of cherrywood, and a ceiling of pressed copper. At each of the booths was a mirror flanked by lamps. However, on Mother's Day in 1955, a fire destroyed this ornamentation. The Basiles rebuilt the business, and it has come to be a Vandergrift icon. Here is Pete Basile cooking for customers. An early menu lists French toast with syrup, butter, and coffee for 60¢ and homemade chili with a roll and butter for 40¢. (Historic image courtesy of Poppy Basile.)

Opposite Sweetlane's grill is an entirely different world. Within these glass cases is an assortment of chocolates that were handmade by Peter and Poppy Basile for Easter, the shop's busiest holiday. Specialties include turtles, dipped cherries, creams, caramels, and peanut butter meltaways. It is hard to miss the large chocolate bunny that takes center stage on the top of the glass display cases. It was molded from one of Poppy's collection of candy molds that were purchased in the United States and Europe. Poppy continues to make chocolates by hand for the shop. (Historic image courtesy of Poppy Basile.)

This building, once located at the corner of Grant and Sumner Avenues, was severely destroyed by a fire. The ground floor portion remains, although modified. Its long-standing occupant, S and T Bank, moved, leaving the space open for Vandergrift's municipal offices and police station. For the duration of Vandergrift's history up until this move, the police station and municipal offices were located in the west wing of the Casino building.

The Penn-Grant Hotel was built around 1908. It is shown here in its most prosperous period, the 1940s. There was a first floor bar known as the Rainbow Room and a second bar on the floor below. A large dining room served reputable food, and a live band performed there at least once a week. In the 1950s, business began to slow, and along with the customers, the building went too. Before it was demolished, it was estimated that it would have cost $175,000 to repair. It was torn down in the 1970s.

The Sherman Inn, shown here around 1900, was built in 28 days. George Gibson McMurtry notified H. W. Nichols, his contractor, on January 31, 1897, that he wanted a suitable place for Vandergrift's visitors to stay, and he wanted it by February 28 of the same year. Amazingly, Nichols accomplished this feat, and the building has withstood being moved from its original location at the corner of Sherman and Washington Avenues to its present location across from the Victorian Vandergrift Museum and Historical Society. It is now a private residence.

Where Hamilton Avenue met Sherman Avenue, H. W. Phillips had a garage and automobile supply shop, shown here in the second decade of the 20th century. Take note of the ornately decorated hearse parked in front. His brick structure has given way to a newer cement block structure. The building may have changed, but the present business still has to do with cars. It is now owned by Greece Lightning Car Wash and Detail Shop.

CHAPTER 4

EVERY MAKE
AND MODEL

Taken on July 4, 1908, this photograph depicts Vandergrift residents at the bottom of the park leading up to the Casino building. It seems that they were very enthusiastic about using this new technology, and their enthusiasm only grew in the future. By the 1950s, Vandergrift boasted 11 car dealerships, and a group known as the Kiski Valley Dealers was organized to unite dealers in Vandergrift and the entire Kiskiminetas Valley.

Riverview Garage, shown here in 1922, was located along Franklin Avenue. In its earliest stage, it sold Nash and Paige cars. From 1922 to 1930, it was owned by Wylie Fitzgerald. Not only was it a car dealership at this time, but it was also a gasoline station and ambulance service. From 1947 until 1949, the site was taken over by Roy Harmon, who sold and repaired Studebakers. The site is now the home of Sprankle's Market.

This Buick dealership was located along Walnut Street. During the 1930s, it was owned by Silas E. Mohney. From 1947 to 1949, it came under the ownership of James Euwer, with Rodney Euwer as the assistant manager. The property then became the site of the Vandergrift Building and Loan Association, which was responsible for the complete transformation in the structure's appearance. This was then taken over by Vandergrift Federal Savings in the late 1980s. In the early 1990s, it became the district justice office.

At one time, a car dealership occupied the building that now houses the Occasions party store and Buttermilk Falls Printing Company, which is responsible for the printing of the Vandergrift newspaper. McCutcheon Auto Company supplied Vandergrift residents with Chevrolet cars. The upper portion of Washington Avenue came to be a showcase of Vandergrift's beautiful house architecture, but here, within the lower portion, businesses were established as George Gibson McMurtry intended.

EVERY MAKE AND MODEL

At one point, this building along Hancock Avenue was the home of W. H. George Automobiles, Auto Supplies, Motor Cycles, and Gas Engines. In 1940, it became Grosser Tire Service, and in 1947, it developed into the business that it appears as for this historic photograph, Guthrie's Chevrolet. Keddie Chevrolet also came to occupy this building before moving to its present site on Lincoln Avenue. On the last change of hands this structure went through, it became Byers Taxi Service.

The Ferrante family initially had a car shop across from Donghia Lumber on Walnut Street. It was opened by Anthony Ferrante on March 1, 1932, and during World War II, it sold Hudson cars. In the mid-1940s, the shop was moved to this site along Jackson Avenue right before it turns into Wallace Street. The Ferrante Motor Company sold Plymouth and Desoto cars here through Chrysler until 1958. (Historic image courtesy of Rosemary Ferrante.)

EVERY MAKE AND MODEL

This image shows the new Ferrante showroom across Jackson Avenue from the company's previous site. The Ferrante Motor Company became an Oldsmobile dealer in 1959, and it is around this time that this image was taken. Many may be surprised that, in such a small town, it would be possible to find Smart Cars and Segways, but anyone passing by Ferrante Motor today will see an array of them for sale. (Historic image courtesy of Rosemary Ferrante.)

Having so many car dealerships to choose from in Vandergrift's earlier and more recent years obviously requires service stations to keep motorists happy. Situated on Holland Avenue before it snakes off into La Belle Vue Road, also known as the Serpentine, Ralph G. Shaffer established a service company in 1930, which is depicted here. William Campbell took over the business in 1947 and named it Campbell's Service Station. Only two years later, August Mangifest bought the station. From the 1950s to the 1980s, it existed as Morgan's Service Station. The building now houses Digital Designs.

EVERY MAKE AND MODEL

5

Day's End in a Workingman's Paradise

The Kiski Theater of 115 Grant Avenue advertises images of Vandergrift, enticing citizens with the line "You may see yourself." Wister Elliot bought the theater from Leonard G. Elswick in May 1922. This made Elliot responsible for at least three of the town's theaters, as he also owned the Star Theater and leased the Casino Theatre. Vandergrift boasted so many theaters that it is hard to imagine that they all would have been filled, even if all of the town's residents tried to go to the movies at the same time. Once the workday was over, these theaters, along with other recreational activities, provided a means of escape for workers, business owners, and their respective families.

This is a slightly later historic image of 115 Grant Avenue, showing it as it appeared in 1953 when it was Manos Theater. *Mogambo*, a movie staring Clark Gable, Ava Gardner, and Grace Kelly, came out that year, and the theater is decorated with *Mogambo* memorabilia. After being a theater for the duration of its early history, it became Fontana's Casa della Porta where Bill Fontana operated a business that produced homemade pasta. It is now Tommy's Catering. Despite the change in the building's purpose from a movie house to food-themed businesses, it still has the theater marquee above the entranceway.

DAY'S END IN A WORKINGMAN'S PARADISE

Built in 1900 according to the design of architect James E. Allison, the Casino is the oldest performing arts theater in southwestern Pennsylvania that is still in operation. The Casino building has also served as the town's library and municipal building. It has been the location of live theater performances, vaudeville, movies, high school graduations, and church services for the town's early congregations. In 1918, former president William Howard Taft became just one presenter of note when he delivered a speech about World War I here. Included among its treasures are stained-glass windows designed by Rudy Brothers Company, which was considered one of Pittsburgh's best glass studios from 1894 to 1920. (Historic image courtesy of Norman Myers.)

When the Victor Emanuel III Sons of Italy lodge dedicated the Sons of Italy building on May 27, 1922, the entire community gained a place for good food and entertainment. Renamed Primo Event Hall by its new owners, James Cibik and David Cable, who bought the old building in September 2007, it has been reopened for events. The historic image shows the larger upstairs hall and stage, which is now about to be remodeled, while the modern image shows the downstairs hall, the Godfather Banquet Room, which was completed in April 2008. (Historic image courtesy of Bonnie McGuire.)

When the mill filled in the Grove in 1919, the level ground created the opportunity for the construction of a baseball park. From 1947 to 1950, a professional baseball team called the Vandergrift Pioneers played here. In their first and second years, the team won the Middle Atlantic Baseball League Championships. Even before the Pioneers, Vandergrift was home to an African American baseball team known as the Grays in the 1920s. (Historic image courtesy of Norman Myers.)

Here is a group of spectators in the stands of Vandergrift's baseball field during the 1920s. Players sit among the fans. With professional baseball's move out of the town, the field was transformed for the use of the Kiski Area High School football team. These stands were located at the south end of the baseball field in the same position as the student section bleachers in what is now Davis Field. The field was named for Stewart A. Davis, who had helped George Gibson McMurtry in his plans for Vandergrift's development. (Historic image courtesy of Norman Myers.)

DAY'S END IN A WORKINGMAN'S PARADISE

6

PREPARING VANDERGRIFT'S FUTURE GENERATIONS

St. Gertrude School's fifth-grade class, taught by Sr. Mary Wilfred, O.S.B., sat for this photograph in 1952. This group of students was the first to go through all eight of the grades offered by the school at the time. In May 1897, Vandergrift's school board was established and began planning for the education of the town's youth. Initial classes were mostly made up of girls, however, since boys began work at an early age. (Historic image courtesy of Carmen Palmer.)

In this photograph, taken on Monday, November 15, 1897, the opening day of the Custer Avenue Public School is shown. The no-admittance boards have only just been removed from the front door, and students and teachers can be seen looking out of the windows. The first class to graduate from this school in 1902 was made up of 15 girls. (Historic image courtesy of the Vandergrift Public Library.)

PREPARING VANDERGRIFT'S FUTURE GENERATIONS

In 1900, Vandergrift's second school, the Lincoln Avenue Public School, was built. It is shown on the right in this historic image with the Custer School just to the left. The Lincoln School had eight classrooms, a gymnasium, and an auditorium that could hold 350. Eventually, it had to serve as a high school until another building for this purpose could be constructed in 1919. Both the Custer and Lincoln Schools have been replaced by Keddie Chevrolet.

Vandergrift's third public school, after the Custer and Lincoln Avenue buildings, was this structure on Sherman Avenue in 1911. It would later become the office space for school district administrators. In 1999, it was purchased by the Victorian Vandergrift Museum and Historical Society (VVMHS), which began to restore the building. The VVMHS has offices, archives, and a public museum here.

PREPARING VANDERGRIFT'S FUTURE GENERATIONS

In this image, a group of students stands just outside the doors of St. Gertrude Catholic School in the 1950s. This building is located just above St. Gertrude Church on Franklin Avenue. On August 24, 1924, during the tenure of Fr. Edgar Zuercher, the school was blessed. In a dedication and blessing ceremony on November 27, 2005, the school was renamed Cardinal Maida Academy. Cardinal Adam J. Maida is a native of East Vandergrift but now serves the diocese in Detroit. (Historic image courtesy of Carmen Palmer.)

Children from Vandergrift Heights started school in a wooden structure located on this site along Longfellow Street in 1898. The Longfellow building was located here and existed just to the left of where this school, the Wilson building, was constructed in 1911. It was named for Woodrow Wilson and existed long after the Longfellow building was torn down. The school came to be used for apartments but was demolished in 2008.

PREPARING VANDERGRIFT'S FUTURE GENERATIONS

Originally, this school was built in 1919 to serve as Vandergrift's high school. The last high school class graduated from here in 1962. At this point, it became Vandergrift Junior High School, accommodating grades seven through nine. Grades 10 through 12 were moved to a new building that was constructed on the site of Vandergrift's airport, which was located one or two miles outside of the town. When an intermediate school was opened on the same site as the new high school in the 1990s, the old high school came to serve as an elementary school.

The runways of the Vandergrift Airport are here viewed from the air. The airport began in 1928 with one airplane on a patch of farmland. It became an airmail station, where planes dropped a parcel of incoming mail, while a hook coming down from the plane picked up the outgoing mail attached to a rope loop suspended by two poles. Kiski Area High School opened on this same site in 1962. The current building is the result of remodeling that was completed in 2005.

PREPARING VANDERGRIFT'S FUTURE GENERATIONS

CHAPTER

7

GOOD CHURCHES
FOR GOOD PEOPLE

To encourage churches to settle in Vandergrift, George Gibson McMurtry offered religious groups a deed for some of Vandergrift's best lots, $7,500 toward a church building if it cost at least $15,000 to build, and a new organ. He felt that the good people of his new town deserved good churches. One of the churches that eventually settled in the town was St. Gertrude Roman Catholic Church, the interior of which is shown in this 1969 photograph. (Historic image courtesy of Bonnie McGuire.)

The First Evangelical Lutheran Church is the result of the efforts of the first group to take George Gibson McMurtry's offer. It cost $16,984.90 to build and was designed in 1896–1897 by Alden and Harlow, Pittsburgh's leading architectural firm from 1896 to 1908. The cornerstone for this building was laid in November 1896, and the dedication took place on June 22, 1897. It was begun with 117 members.

In June 1896, Apollo Presbyterians were given permission to establish a church in Vandergrift. The cornerstone was laid for the First Presbyterian Church in April 1897. Services were first held here in September of that year. In 1896, United Presbyterians from Apollo and Vandergrift began holding services led by Rev. R. A. Jamison in private homes. The First Presbyterian Church offered its sanctuary to this growing congregation until its church, which became Trinity United, was finished in 1898. First Presbyterian and Trinity United came together again when the two churches merged on July 7, 2002. The church is now led by Rev. F. Neal Galley.

The rounded arches of the original tower, windows, and entry contribute to the Romanesque style of the First United Methodist Church. Architect James E. Allison was responsible for its design, and the cornerstone was put into place on July 1, 1897. Rev. Noble G. Miller was part of the organizing force for the church in September of the previous year. This church group held its first service in their new building on Valentine's Day in 1898. Structural additions were made in 1958–1959.

GOOD CHURCHES FOR GOOD PEOPLE

St. Gertrude's Roman Catholic Church, completed in 1912 and now on the National Register of Historic Places, is much grander than the small church that the congregation began worshipping in during April 1898. John T. Comes designed the Romanesque-style church that now stands on Franklin Avenue. George W. Sotter, a well-known Pittsburgh painter and stained-glass artist who lived from 1879 to 1953, was responsible for the clerestory windows.

The First Baptist Church of Vandergrift began as a mission of the First Baptist Church of Apollo, but on October 8, 1899, the worshippers decided to establish their own church in Vandergrift. The final structure is viewed here at the corner of Adams and Franklin Avenues. The Franklin Avenue bridge (right) can be seen in the historic photograph. This bridge passed over a railroad cut that was filled in by the foundry in the 1920s, creating the small park stretching from Hancock to Franklin Avenues.

GOOD CHURCHES FOR GOOD PEOPLE

Here is an interior view of the First Reformed Church of the United Church of Christ. This church's initial congregation was organized on August 27, 1899, in the United Presbyterian Church. The group purchased land on Franklin Avenue where they continued to worship in a small wooden chapel from December 23, 1900, until a few days before the dedication of the present church building on March 23, 1902. Geyer and Mowbray of Greensburg were the architects.

Rev. John W. Poffinberger, who was responsible for the organization of the First Evangelical Lutheran Church, began a church school around 1901 in Vandergrift Heights. By May of the following year, this school had developed into St. Paul's Lutheran Church. The initial congregation of 69 members erected a building at the corner of Emerson and Walnut Streets. Rev. George Beiswanger became the new leader for the group in their new building.

In April 1914, members of SS. Constantine and Helen Greek Orthodox Church purchased land on Lincoln Avenue. They began construction of their church in 1916. By 1920, the congregation numbered about 250. The last full regular services were held here sometime in the late 1960s or early 1970s. Today a Greek Orthodox priest from New Kensington comes to the church to perform sacramental ceremonies. The altarpiece appears here with icons imported from Greece and other works done by immigrant Greek craftsmen.

This is an image of the Franklin Avenue Church of God, dedicated in 1921. Rev. J. T. Lackey contributed much to this church after becoming pastor in June 1932. He was also responsible for the organization of the Vandergrift Ministerial Association. When additions were made to the back of the church, the altar was moved to the side that was originally the entrance. Behind this altar is a beautiful stained-glass window. The congregation now numbers 125 and has been led since 2006 by Rev. Kathleen Taylor. They are a truly welcoming group, representative of the sense of community that Vandergrift has to offer. (Historic image courtesy of Rev. Kathleen Taylor.)

BIBLIOGRAPHY

The Fiftieth Anniversary of the First Baptist Church and Parsonage. Vandergrift, PA: 1950.

History of the First United Presbyterian Church of Vandergrift Pennsylvania. Vandergrift, PA.

Homecoming. Vandergrift, PA: Franklin Avenue Church of God, 1971.

"Old Hotel Succumbs to Time." *Valley News Dispatch.* February 14, 1974.

Scott, Cora Lee. "Sweetlane Chocolate Shop." *Vandergrift News.* February 10, 1999.

Something Better Than the Best. Vandergrift, PA: 1995 Centennial Committee, Inc. and the Victorian Vandergrift Museum and Historical Society, 1996.

St. Gertrude Church Golden Jubilee. Vandergrift, PA: 1948.

Tarbell, Ida M. *New Ideals in Business: An Account of Their Practice and Their Effects Upon Men and Profits.* New York: Macmillan, 1916.

Vandergrift Pennsylvania. Vandergrift, PA: Vandergrift Chamber of Commerce.

Zufelt, Jerry. "The Cardinal Maida Academy." The *Catholic Accent.* December 8, 2005.

ACROSS AMERICA, PEOPLE ARE DISCOVERING SOMETHING WONDERFUL. *THEIR HERITAGE.*

Arcadia Publishing is the leading local history publisher in the United States. With more than 3,000 titles in print and hundreds of new titles released every year, Arcadia has extensive specialized experience chronicling the history of communities and celebrating America's hidden stories, bringing to life the people, places, and events from the past. To discover the history of other communities across the nation, please visit:

www.arcadiapublishing.com

Customized search tools allow you to find regional history books about the town where you grew up, the cities where your friends and family live, the town where your parents met, or even that retirement spot you've been dreaming about.